STONEHENGE
AND HISTORIC WESSEX

ENGLISH HERITAGE

Dorchester

'Compact as a box of dominoes' is how writer and poet Thomas Hardy (1840–1928) described the town he lived in, and loved, and wove into so many of his Wessex stories as 'Casterbridge'. Roman town-planning is responsible for Dorchester's layout but, before you explore the town, visit **The Dorset County Museum** . This

treasure house, with its wonderful **Roman mosaics** and many fascinating discoveries from Dorset's earlier history, will quickly show you the richness of Dorchester's past. Up the hill from the museum is the Shire Hall containing the Old Crown Court. Look out for the plaque dedicated to the **Tolpuddle Martyrs** , six agricultural labourers who were tried here on 17 March 1834 for forming a trade union, and sentenced to transportation!

A hundred-and-fifty years earlier the infamous Judge Jeffreys had presided over another unhappy landmark in legal history: the Bloody

Judge Jeffreys of the Bloody Assize.

Assize. Of the 300 followers of the Duke of Monmouth who were tried here, many received the death sentence: the heads of some were put on public display outside **St Peter's Church** ☐ (next to the museum) as a grisly warning. The executioner was kept busy in Dorchester, and you can still see **Hangman's Cottage** ☐ where he rested between engagements. **Maumbury Rings** ☐ – the Stone Age earthwork converted to a gladiatorial arena by the Romans – is another place with unhappy memories, but not all Dorchester history is dark. At Top o' Town is the **Thomas Hardy statue** ☐. From here you can explore the tree-lined **West Walks** ☐, which follows the Roman wall, or visit the **Roman Town House** ☐ in Colliton Park.

The Cerne Abbas Giant.

Thomas Hardy's short story 'The Withered Arm' from *Wessex Tales* features the Hangman's Cottage, and *The Mayor of Casterbridge* is set in the town. You may want to visit the cottage in Higher Bockhampton where Hardy was born (Tel. 01305 262366) or the house he built for himself at Max Gate near Dorchester (Tel. 01305 262538). Dorset County Museum, Higher West Street is open all year Mon-Sat (and Sun in July and August) 10.00 am to 5.00 pm. Everyone visiting Dorchester should also see Maiden Castle 2 miles from the town. The **Cerne Abbas Giant** ☐ – a rather rude chalk figure which may or may not be a giant cartoon of the Roman Emperor Commodus (AD 161–192) who was proud of his muscles and dressed up as Hercules – is always worth a visit. He is about 6 miles north on the A352 Sherborne road.

Maiden Castle

When you visit Maiden Castle, climb to the top and look around you at the defensive ditches and **earth ramparts** of one of the greatest Iron Age hill forts in Europe. Think back to AD 44 when this was the headquarters of a Celtic tribe called the Durotriges, and a formidable fortress. The Celts had perfected the slingshot as a weapon and had vast stores of ammunition (pebbles from Chesil Beach) within the inner circle. A deadly rain of these missiles could cut down attackers as they scrambled up the slippery, exposed slopes. But it is unlikely that the Celts felt secure in their huts early on a

certain day in AD 44. Ranged against them was the most efficient war machine the world had ever seen: the Roman Army. At the head of his crack regiment, the 2nd Augusta legion, was an able general who was one day to become Emperor of Rome: Vespasian.

Can you imagine what it was like that day? Archaeology has revealed a grim story. Vespasian judged that the eastern gate was the weak point. He attacked with ballistae (great military catapults), the heavy bolts smashing the barricade. A bolt has been found lodged in the spine of a defender's skeleton. Celtic men, women, and children poured into the breach but the Roman infantry moved remorselessly forward reaping a bloody harvest with their short swords. The terrible injuries that can be seen on the skeletons which have been found tell the rest of the story, and the pall of white ash which covered the summit of Maiden Castle after the huts were burned. Back in Rome, the Emperor Claudius was given a victory parade for his generals' successes in Britain.

> Maiden Castle is 2 miles south of Dorchester off the A354, south of the bypass. It can be visited at any reasonable time.

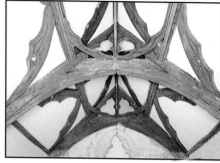

Fiddleford Mill

This medieval manor house is famed for the craftsmanship of its **magnificent roof**. Originally built in the fourteenth century, in the sixteenth century the house belonged to Thomas and Ann White. In making alterations to their home, they had their **initials** incorporated by the workmen. How many can you find?

Jordan Hill Roman Temple, Weymouth

As you travel through the lanes of Dorset, you are likely to see **starlings** and **crows**, and even **ravens** and the occasional **buzzard**. Try to imagine what dark ritual prompted Romanized Celts of the fourth century AD to bury numerous skeletons of these birds, each with a small coin, in a deep shaft below the foundations of this mysterious building overlooking Weymouth Bay.

Kingston Russell Stone Circle

In 1815 one of the stones in this **circle**, which dates back as far as 3000 years, was still standing – now they have all fallen. Can you find **all eighteen stones**?

Knowlton Church and Earthworks

A ruined Norman church stands surrounded by 35 round barrows: a Christian island in a sea of pagan burial sites.

Fiddleford Mill is 1 mile east of Sturminster Newton off the A357.
    Open daily 1 April–31 Oct 10 am–6 pm
    1 Nov–31 March 10 am–4 pm
    (Closed 24-26 Dec, 1 Jan)

Jordan Hill Roman Temple is 2 miles north-east of Weymouth off the A353. It can be visited at any reasonable time.

Kingston Russell Stone Circle is 2 miles north of Abbotsbury, 1 mile along a footpath off a minor road to the Hardy Monument – any reasonable time. Visit the memorial to Admiral Hardy, one of three Dorset captains at the Battle of Trafalgar. Nelson did indeed say 'Kiss me Hardy'; it was a touching farewell between close friends when he knew he was about to die.

Knowlton Church is 3 miles south-west of Cranborne on the B3078. Any reasonable time.

Lulworth Castle ☐

Despite its austere military appearance, Lulworth (*left*) – built as a hunting lodge in 1609 – has never seen any fighting: unless it was among the Weld family over questions of fashion during its eighteenth-century transformation into an elegant country house. Look for the **Weld arms** ☐ over the main door, and the beautiful **formal garden** ☐ (*below left*).

Portland Castle ☐ (*below*)

The best preserved of all Henry VIII's coastal forts still frowns across Weymouth Bay, its bald head of Portland stone recalling the pugnacious features of the monarch who defied the French and Spanish to invade his England.

Sherborne Old Castle ☐

If Lulworth is a building dreaming of being a castle, then battle-scarred Sherborne is the real thing. The castle had already seen five centuries of turbulent history when, in 1642, it was held for King Charles I in the Civil War. Still defiant, in 1645 Sherborne again refused to abandon its king. This time Fairfax – the 'rebels' new brutish general' – cut down the old warrior with cannon: it took him sixteen days.

Sherborne Old Castle (above) and King Charles I (left)

Lulworth Castle lies in East Lulworth off the B3070, 3 miles north-east of Lulworth Cove
Open 30 March–31 Oct, daily 10 am–6 pm
1 Nov–22 Dec daily 10 am–4 pm

Portland Castle is next to the Royal Navy helicopter base overlooking Portland Harbour
open daily 1 April–31 Oct, 10 am–6 pm

Sherborne Old Castle is ½ mile east of Sherborne off the B3145.
Open 1 April–31 Oct, daily 10 am–6 pm
1 Nov–31 March, Wed-Sun 10 am–4 pm
(closed 24–26 Dec, 1 Jan)

Farleigh Hungerford Castle ☐
Sir Thomas Hungerford lies buried in the fine chapel of the castle he and his son built in the late fourteenth century. Look for the **wall paintings** ☐ and **stained glass** ☐. The two great towers of the now ruined castle are still impressive.

Glastonbury Tribunal
This **medieval townhouse** ☐ was once the courthouse of the Abbots of Glastonbury, becoming a private dwelling after the Dissolution of the Monasteries. It houses a museum and the Tourist Information Centre and is an excellent place to begin your exploration of Glastonbury. See the **Abbey** ☐ and the miraculous thorn said to have grown from the staff of Joseph of Arimathaea.

Glastonbury Tribunal

The **Glastonbury Thorn** ☐ flowers at Christmas and again at Easter: in some legends it is even said to have come from Christ's Crown of Thorns.

The ground floor chamber of Glastonbury Tribunal

There is a tradition that King Arthur is associated with Glastonbury and its famous **Tor** ☐. All too often, Arthur is depicted wearing medieval armour. In the illustration (*right*) the artist has portrayed him as the Romano-Celtic chieftain he would have been.

Farleigh Hungerford Castle is 3½ miles west of Trowbridge on the A366.
Open daily 1 April–31 Oct 10 am–6 pm
1 Nov–31 March, Wed–Sun 10 am – 4 pm
(Closed 24-26 Dec, 1 Jan)

Glastonbury Tribunal is in Glastonbury High Street.
Open daily 1 April–30 Sep 10 am–5 pm
(6 pm on Friday and Saturday)
1 Oct–31 March 10 am–4 pm

Muchelney Abbey

It was no hollow boast when the king's secretary, Thomas Cromwell, promised to make Henry VIII 'the richest prince in Christendom' by seizing Church property – the Dissolution of the Monasteries. Founded in AD 762, and re-established by King Athelstan in AD 937, Muchelney Abbey was one of hundreds destroyed between 1536 and 1539. Cromwell's bullies arrived at Muchelney, and the Benedictine monks said prayers for the last time, in 1538. The **Abbot's Lodging** is well preserved through being used as a farmhouse; the **cloisters** of honeyed stone dream peacefully.

Thomas Cromwell, brutal architect of the Dissolution of the Monasteries.

Nunney Castle

This small, moated castle, built by Sir Elias de la Mere in the fourteenth century, saw service throughout the Civil War. The four-storey central block with a round tower at each corner is a design more often found in France.

Muchelney Abbey lies 2 miles south of Langport
Open daily, 10 am–6 pm 1 April–30 Sep 10 am–5 pm

Nunney Castle is 3½ miles south-west of Frome, off the A361.
Open all the year round.

Salisbury

The height of its steeple
The pride of its people
Its scissors and knives
And diligent wives

The old rhyme about Salisbury gives a good idea of a rich medieval town with prosperous merchant guilds flourishing in the shadow of its great cathedral. As commerce became more important than defence, and an expanding population demanded a regular water supply, New Sarum (still Salisbury's official name) eclipsed Old Sarum – a new town and a new cathedral springing up on the immense profits from the wool trade.

Begin your exploration of Salisbury at the **Cathedral** dedicated to St Mary. The foundation stones for this glorious building were laid in 1220; it was completed 38 years later. The **spire** was added early in the fourteenth century – at 404 feet (123.14 m) the tallest in Britain. Cathedral treasures include the **Magna Carta** , sealed at Runnymede on 15 June 1215, and the oldest working **clock** in England.

Your next stop in Salisbury should be the **King's House** in the Cathedral Close; it contains the marvellous Salisbury and South Wiltshire Museum. In addition to many fascinating exhibitions on all aspects of the city's past, this also houses the **Stonehenge Gallery** and the spectacular **Monkton Deverill gold torc** .

On leaving the King's House, explore the wonders of the **Cathedral Close** , including **Malmesbury House** (*opposite left*) before venturing into the town. Look out for the 600-year-old **Poultry Cross** (*above*) and the **Parish Church of St Thomas à Becket** with its famous **Doom Painting** .

Salisbury and South Wiltshire Museum
 Open Mon–Sat 10 am–5 pm. In July and August
 and during the Salisbury Festival also Sunday 2 pm–5 pm

All visitors to New Sarum (Salisbury) should visit Old Sarum just 2 miles away (*see* next pages)

Nell Gwyn (opposite right) received a fabulously expensive set of Salisbury cutlery from her royal lover Charles II.

Old Sarum

Old Sarum is a haunted place – a windswept hilltop on which men and women have lived for 5000 years, but now a place for picnickers and birds. In its heyday 800 years ago, it boasted a royal palace, a castle, and the first Salisbury Cathedral. It was here, in 1070, that William of Normandy summoned and paid off the troops who had made him 'William the Conqueror' and won England for him. When you visit Old Sarum, climb up and find a comfortable place to sit. Think of the grassy circle within a circle as a great natural time machine – because that is what it is really.

First go back 5000 years. It is the Stone Age. All around the hill, thick forest stretches as far as the eye can see. Here and there the first farmers are clearing the forest: thin grey smoke rises from their fires. Many people have settled on this natural hill to protect their cattle and themselves from wolves and bears: their huts cluster around you.

Now move forward in time, quickly, and as the centuries fly past, more and more of the forest is cut down. Stop! It is the Iron Age, around 500 BC. An outer bank has been constructed around the hill for better protection. Old Sarum has grown wealthy in cattle and it is now other people who must be kept out. Warfare has arrived.

Move forward in time again, but more slowly, only five centuries will pass. First the Romans come and conquer the Celts: they build on the hill and their straight roads intersect at Old Sarum. The Romans leave and the Saxons come, pushing the Celts to the west. A Saxon town is built around you, so strong the Vikings cannot take Old Sarum. But now it is 1066 and the Normans come, and they do take the town.

Come forward now to the present day. We will go to see what remains of Norman Old Sarum.

Old Sarum is 2 miles north of Salisbury off the A345
Open daily 1 April–31 Oct 10 am–6 pm
1 Nov–31 March 10 am–4 pm
(closed 24-26 Dec, 1 Jan)

Old Sarum

If you look around, you will see the **outer bank** ___ of the Iron Age fort, and, at the centre, the raised mound of the **inner bailey** ___ of the Norman Castle. As you enter the inner stronghold, to your right are the foundations of the **Royal Palace** ___. Straight ahead are the remains of the **keep** ___ or great tower. Return now to the **outer bailey** ___, the area between the central mound and the outer Iron Age bank. To the north, clearly visible in the grass, you will find the foundations of the great cathedral built by

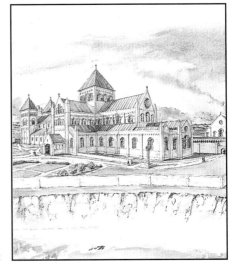

Bishop Roger. This incorporated parts of the earlier cathedral built by Bishop Osmund – St Osmund, said to be William the Conqueror's nephew. The first cathedral was consecrated in 1092 but, only five days later, it was damaged by a great storm.

As you leave, you can find some relics of more recent invasion threats that Old Sarum has withstood – the **lavatories** in the car park are built on the site of a World War II machine gun post. If you are careful, and cross the main road where the entrance lane leaves it, you may see a boulder in the hedge to the left. This marks the baseline of the original Ordnance Survey of 1794: good maps were essential if England was to defend itself against Napoleon!

A memorial of a different kind can be found if you return to the East Gate main entrance and take the fenced footpath to the right where the road bends sharply. Turn right at the open field. A stone marker beyond the stile commemorates William Pitt the Younger (1759–1806): a great Prime Minister elected by dubious means. Old Sarum's sad end was as England's most notorious 'rotten borough' where it took only two voters to elect a member of Parliament.

Avebury

To visit Avebury is to take a trip back to the Stone Age. All the monuments at Avebury – one of the most complete prehistoric sites in Europe – date from between 6000 and 4000 years ago. We know that early people – who lived by hunting and gathering plants – were in the area even before that, in the period following the last ice age 10,000 to 7000 years ago. But it is farmers who build things: they have the time, knowing that they can be sure of feeding themselves, and they have learned to co-operate with one another.

There is a fascinating museum of prehistory at Avebury. Alexander Keiller was a talented amateur archaeologist who spent a considerable fortune in the 1930s discovering and restoring the secrets of Avebury. The next time you see another kind of preserve, **Dundee Marmalade**, remember we owe it all to that – and to one man's enthusiasm.

But before the **museum**, explore Avebury itself! We will start with the oldest monument.

Windmill Hill

Windmill Hill seems to have been used as a seasonal meeting place around 3700 BC. In spring and autumn, people from a wide area gathered to exchange goods such as stone axes and pottery. Bone fragments show that animals were slaughtered as well as traded at these great seasonal fairs. More gruesome are the human remains that have been found, including those of a child: relics of strange ceremonies and rituals long forgotten.

The Alexander Keiller Museum
  open daily 1 April–31 Oct 10 am–6 pm
  1 Nov–31 March, Wed–Sun 10 am–4 pm
  (Closed 24–26 Dec, 1 Jan)

Windmill Hill is 1½ miles north-west of Avebury and accessible at any reasonable time.

West Kennet Long Barrow

West Kennet Long Barrow is a vast communal tomb used continuously from as early as 3700 BC to around 2000 BC. Look for the **three upright stones** which blocked the entrance. Although a complete skeleton of an elderly man killed by an arrow in the throat has been found, most of the bones are separate and either sorted into piles or jumbled up. The absence of many individual bones, especially skulls and long bones, may be linked to the findings at Windmill Hill. We can only guess at what our distant ancestors did with these grim relics of their dead, and what supernatural powers they were believed to possess.

West Kennet Long Barrow is situated ½ mile south-west of West Kennet along a footpath off the A4. It can be visited at any reasonable time.

Avebury Stone Circles

The Avebury Circles are the largest in Britain. Constructed 4000 years ago, they originally comprised 180 sarsen stones, many weighing over 20 tonnes each. The Avebury Circles are still an awesome sight, and there is evidence that even Roman tourists came to marvel at them. The invading Saxons called this wonder of prehistory, *Weala-dic*, 'the moat of the British'. The Saxons built a long house where the modern car park

now is, and the village that later developed is completely encircled by the **ditch and bank**, surmounted by its ancient, brooding stones.

Avebury is situated 7 miles west of Marlborough
The stone circles can be visited at any reasonable time.

The Sanctuary   West Kennet Avenue

Connecting Avebury's stone circles with the other mysterious circular structure, known as The Sanctuary, is West Kennet Avenue (*see* opposite). Originally, this consisted of more than 100 pairs of upright stones. The eighteenth-century antiquarian William Stukeley likened the curves of the Avenue to a snake: why its builders of 4000 years ago did not make it straight we may never know.

What was The Sanctuary? A considerable amount of human bone has been found within its concentric circles, and it clearly marks an important spot. The earliest, inner circle (around 3000 BC) was of wood; other circles of wood and stone were added later. Is the burial of a young man with a beaker, discovered

at The Sanctuary, evidence of human sacrifice? Again, we may never know.

But the greatest mystery of all at Avebury is **Silbury Hill** . This is the largest artificial mound in Europe, the same size as Egypt's smaller pyramids. In 1922, the Egyptologist Flinders Petrie bored a tunnel expecting to find a burial chamber: he was disappointed. Why did people build Silbury Hill? With simple stone, bone, and wooden tools they excavated 350,000 cubic metres of chalk and soil. It has been calculated that it would have taken 18 million working hours, that is 700 individuals working for ten years! Why?

Opposite: *the building of Silbury Hill.*

West Kennet Avenue runs alongside the B4003. It can be visited at any reasonable time.

The Sanctuary lies beside the A4, ½ mile east of West Kennet.

Silbury Hill cannot be climbed. It can be viewed 1 mile west of West Kennet on the A4. It can be visited at any reasonable time.

Bradford-on-Avon Tithe Barn

The idea that a farmer should give one-tenth – a tithe – of all he produced for the support of the priesthood and of religious establishments goes right back to the Bible. In medieval England this produce was stored in giant tithe barns. The magnificent fourteenth-century tithe barn in Bradford supplied the

Nunnery of Shaftesbury. The massive roof, divided into **fourteen bays**, is still intact. Two of the giant arched supports are true **crucks** – can you see the difference?

Chisbury Chapel

This little chapel, dedicated to St Martin, was built in the late thirteenth century. Until it was rescued, it had been used as a barn. Look for the **thatched roof** restored during World War II.

Ludgershall Castle and Cross

The castle has had royal connections since the turbulent reign of King Stephen (1135–54) and the bitter feud with his fearsome relative, the Empress Matilda of Germany. The late medieval cross is in the main street.

Bradford-on-Avon Tithe Barn is ¼ mile south of the town centre off the B3109. open daily 1 April–31 Oct 10.30 am–5 pm, 1 Nov–31 March 10.30 am–4 pm (closed Christmas Day)

Chisbury Chapel is on an unclassified road off the A4 6 miles east of Marlborough. It can be visited at any reasonable time.

Ludgershall Castle is on the north side of Ludgershall off the A342 and can be visited all the year round.

The Industrial Revolution of the eighteenth and nineteenth centuries changed the face of the world. Britain was the first to experience this baptism of fire and all the economic and social changes that followed. It is exciting that two of the best examples of the advancing Industrial Revolution can still be visited in Wiltshire: and rather sad that one was directly responsible for killing the other.

The **Kennet and Avon Canal**, passing through some of the most beautiful countryside in England, is wonderful to visit today and full of possibilities for recreation of all kinds. But it was created only for business, the business of moving heavy goods – like Welsh slate and coal – from Bristol to London. There are things to see all along the Kennet and Avon, none more impressive than the flight of 29 locks at Devizes where the engineer, John Rennie, raised the canal 237 feet (72.2 m) in 2 miles!

The **Great Western Railway** – the GWR, 'God's Wonderful Railway' – opened on 30 June 1841. The first train ran from Paddington Station in London to Bristol in

The Kennet & Avon Canal Trust has an interesting exhibition at the Canal Centre, Couch Lane, Devizes. Here you can find out about the many ways of enjoying the canal.
　　Open 10 am–5 pm March to Christmas, Tel 01380 721279

While in Devizes, visit The Wiltshire Archaeological Museum at 41 Long Street. It is full of interesting exhibits from Stonehenge and elsewhere.
　　Open 10 am–5 pm, Mon–Sat (closed Bank Holidays and 24-26 Dec and 1 Jan.

The Great Western Railway Museum, Faringdon Road, Swindon, Tel 01793 493189
　　Open Mon–Sat, 10 am–5 pm, Sun 2 pm–5 pm (last admission 4.30 pm)

just four hours. The GWR was the creation of one of the giants of the Victorian age, Isambard Kingdom Brunel (1806–59): many would say it is his greatest achievement. Today, we can still leave Paddington and 'Speed to the West', as hordes of happy holidaymakers did between the wars in the distinctive 'chocolate and cream' carriages. Or we can visit the GWR museum in Swindon, the town the GWR created.

Old Wardour Castle

This romantic castle, with its echoes of France, was built by Lord Lovel in the fourteenth century when he returned from the Hundred Years' War. One of the few places in England where the 'old religion' – Roman Catholicism – was practised without break, the castle was inevitably crushed between the opposing forces in the Civil War. Despite the **war-damaged south-western side**, the castle has many fine features. Look for the **Renaissance entrance** to the hall with the **Arundell Coat of Arms** above. In the gardens you can find a **grotto** and a **miniature Avebury Circle**. Facing the lake there is a **Gothic Pavilion** and nearby a fine **three-seater lavatory** in a 'necessary house'.

Old Wardour Castle is off the A30, 2 miles south-west of Tisbury.
    Open daily from 1 April–31 Oct 10 am–6 pm; 1 Nov–31 March, Wed–Sun 10 am–4 pm (closed 24-26 Dec and 1 Jan)
There is an exhibition on the ground floor about the Civil War.

Stonehenge

The first time you see the great stone circle rising out of Salisbury Plain is an unforgettable moment. When you come near to the circle, you know that where you are standing has been a special place for at least 5000 years: from the beginning of human history.

Nobody knows all the secrets of this mysterious place but, as you walk around

Stonehenge, you can look for some of the clues (use the map with your ticket). Find the **Heel Stone** (*left*). At midsummer, the rising sun aligns with this and shines right into the centre of the circle. Stonehenge was built by farmers. The seasons – changing as the sun's power waxed and waned – were life and death to them. But why build such a massive structure simply to predict the turning point of the year when a simple arrangement of posts would have done the same thing? Obviously, this was a very special event for them, and many people gathered to

celebrate it in some way. We know from human behaviour elsewhere that the sun is very often worshipped as a god – it must be right to call Stonehenge a temple.

Find the **Slaughter Stone**. Did blood sacrifice form part of the ritual? We know from Roman writers that the Druids were bloodthirsty. Forget the Druids – when they arrived, Stonehenge was probably already in ruins. And the so-called Slaughter Stone was once an upright. But the sacrifice of animals may have been involved. Human sacrifice? There is very little evidence for this although, at **Woodhenge**, excavations revealed the skeleton of a child whose skull had been split open.

Stonehenge

The exceptional photograph of Stonehenge in the snow (*right*) reveals many important features. Can you see the **circular bank and ditch** ☐ of the earliest construction before 3000 BC? Also visible are the **station stones** ☐, but their purpose is not known, and the **Avenue** ☐ which seems to be a processional way extending in the direction of the midsummer sunrise. Turn to the next page to find out about the Trilithons and Bluestones, but can you see the circular **South Barrow** ☐?

All around Stonehenge are the round barrow burial mounds of the Bronze Age dead, and the earlier communal Long Barrows of the Stone Age. After you have learned about the construction of Stonehenge (next page), follow the National Trust waymarks from the carpark to find **Old King Barrow** ☐ and **New King Barrow** ☐ (round barrows), and **Winterbourne Stoke** ☐ a well-preserved long barrow. At the same time, you can explore the mysterious **Cursus** ☐ (*top*). Nobody knows the function of this curious elongated track, older even than Stonehenge. Why do the dead cluster all around Stonehenge? Is it simply because it was an important tribal centre and religious site? Or is there some other link we cannot even guess at?

Stonehenge

Stonehenge's **outer ring** ☐ of giant stones joined with **lintels** ☐ is made from sarsen, a hard sandstone, brought from the Marlborough Downs 20 miles away around 2000 BC. Originally there were thirty uprights, each about 25 tonnes, and thirty lintels of 7 tonnes. Inside was a horseshoe shape of five giant trilithons (two uprights weighing up to 45 tonnes each and a huge lintel). These were also of sarsen. You can see that the **surface was dressed** ☐ to make it smoother (unique to Stonehenge), and the giant pieces joined like wood with **mortise and tenon joints** ☐.

If you look carefully, you will see a **collapsed circle** ☐ of smaller stones and a similar **inner horseshoe** ☐. These are the famous **bluestones** ☐, the remnants of an earlier monument on the same site. Incredibly, the original eighty bluestones, weighing 4 tonnes each, were brought 240 miles from the Preseli Mountains in Wales! Some bluestones are known to have been transported to the area as early as 2900 BC. Look for the **groove** ☐ on one of

them indicating that it was part of an earlier structure.

What special significance the bluestones had and why the earliest inhabitants of these islands expended so much effort on this special site over more than 1000 years are secrets buried – perhaps forever – with the countless dead whose burial mounds cluster around Stonehenge.

Stonehenge lies 2 miles west of Amesbury on the junction of the A303 and A344/A360.
  Open daily 1 April–31 Oct
  10 am–6 pm
  1 Nov–31 March 10 am–4 pm
  (closed 24-26 Dec and 1 Jan)

Woodhenge is 1½ miles north of Amesbury off the A345 just south of Durrington.
  Open at any reasonable time.

Winchester

More than in any other great English city, it is Winchester's imposing **cathedral** which is the key to understanding its history. From AD 662 until today, the succession of the Bishops of Winchester is unbroken. In 871 Alfred the Great – one of a short list of kings who really deserved to be called Great – made Winchester the capital of his Christian kingdom of Wessex, and so effectively capital of England. It was to Winchester that William the Conqueror came to claim his crown in 1066, and here the Domesday Book was compiled. Visit the cathedral before exploring the city. Find the **tomb of William of Wykeham** (*top right*) founder of Winchester College; the **memorial window of Izaac Walton** author of *The Compleat Angler*, and the simple **grave of Jane Austen** . The Visitor's Centre in the Inner Close and the nearby City Museum in the Square are good places to find out where in the city to explore next.

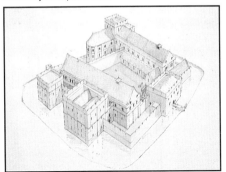

(Above) 'Bloody' Mary Tudor. (Left) Old Bishop's Palace, Wolvesey.

Wolvesey: Old Bishop's Palace

In the vast ruins of Wolvesey – one of the greatest medieval buildings in England – we catch a glimpse of the immense wealth and power of the Bishops of Winchester. Kings and queens were frequent visitors; Philip of Spain and Mary Tudor held their wedding feast here; and in Wolvesey the French ambassadors failed to prevent Henry V's invasion of France which led to the Battle of Agincourt.

Henry V.

Bishop's Waltham Palace

Situated some 6 miles from the city of Winchester, this palace is set in wooded grounds. An exhibition explains the extraordinary history of the Winchester see, until 1929 'reaching from the banks of the Thames to within sight of the coast of France'.

Winchester City Museum, The Square
    Mon–Fri 10 am–5 pm; Sat 10 am–1 pm and 2 pm–5 pm; Sun 2 pm–5 pm
    (closed Mon, Oct–March inc.)

Wolvesey is ¼ mile south-east of the cathedral. Access from College Street.
    Open daily 1 April–31 Oct 10 am–6 pm

Bishop's Waltham Palace is in Bishop's Waltham
    Open daily 1 April–30 Sep 10 am–6 pm

Calshot Castle

On 18 March 1539, the Earl of Southampton and Lord St John decided to deny the French access to the deep-water channel to Southampton by building a gun tower on the shingle spit. A temporary battery was installed immediately, and the highly effective, three-storey, stone tower was completed by the following autumn. Calshot has **loopholes** – dumb-bell-shaped gun windows – can you find them?

The Grange, Northington

The original house was built by Inigo Jones and had **gardens** landscaped by Robert Adam; it was once rented by George IV. Members of two banking families – the Drummonds and then the Barings – made many changes, finally adding the vast **classical portico** said to be a copy of the Temple of Theseus in Athens.

Hurst Castle

One of Henry VIII's largest coastal fortresses, Hurst Castle has had an eventful history. It was the last prison of King Charles I before his trial. A series of unsuitable captains manned it in the seventeenth century: one was caught smuggling tobacco, another arrested for murder. Realizing its strategic importance – controlling the fast current past The Needles – the Victorians armoured Hurst in granite and gave it considerable fire power, including a **38-ton, rifled muzzle-loader**. A submarine telegraph once linked the castle to London and to Queen Victoria's Isle of Wight residence, Osborne.

Henry VIII.

Calshot Castle is on the spit 2 miles south-east of Fawley off the B3053
    Open daily 1 April–30 Sep 10 am–6 pm

The Grange is 4 miles north of New Alresford off the B3046
    Exterior viewing only, at any reasonable time

Hurst Castle is on the pebble spit south of Keyhaven
    Best approached by ferry from Keyhaven
    Open daily 1 April–31 Oct 10 am–6 pm; 1 Nov–31 March 10 am–4 pm weekends only; (closed 24-26 Dec and 1 Jan)

Medieval Merchant's House, Southampton ☐

Imagining 'how it was to live then' is what brings history alive. The house and shop of the thirteenth-century wine merchant, John Fortin, have been carefully restored so that you can do just that.

Netley Abbey ☐

The Abbey, in its beautiful setting, is peaceful again now. Its later history is typical of the fate of many smaller monasteries seized by Henry VIII. In 1536 he gave Netley as a reward to Sir William Paulet. This crafty courtier – who

survived three reigns – converted the abbey to a house. By the eighteenth century, it had been sold and re-sold, mortgaged to pay debts, and fallen into decay. The **North Transept of the Church is now missing** because it was taken to make a garden folly. In the early nineteenth century, the entire building was sold to a Southampton carpenter who stripped the roof and pulled down walls for salvage. The vandalism was profitable, although the carpenter dreamed that he was doomed because of his sacrilege. This proved correct: while he was hacking at the **West Wall**, one of the beautiful tracery windows fell on him and stopped work for good.

If you replace the missing transept in your mind's eye, you can see that the church was built in the shape of a cross; this design is typical of the Cistercians who founded Netley. There are inscriptions on the bases of three of the **great piers** at the transept crossing which record that the Abbey was originally built by Henry III (1207–72).

The Medieval Merchant's House is at 58 French Street, Southampton ¼ mile south of the city centre just off Castle Way (between High Street and Bugle Street)
Open daily 1 April–31 Oct 10 am–6 pm

Netley Abbey is 4 miles south-east of Southampton facing Southampton Water.
It can be viewed at any reasonable time.

Portchester Castle

Built to protect the natural harbour from pirate raids in the third century, the great **Roman walls** of Portchester Castle are the most complete in Europe. Fourteen of the original twenty **bastions** are still standing. In the twelfth century the Roman fortress was transformed into a medieval castle by the addition of a **keep** and an **inner bailey** and **moat**. King Richard II liked Portchester and built a comfortable **royal palace** for himself within the walls. In later centuries, Portchester was used as a prison for important captives and as a military prison during the Napoleonic Wars.

William Shakespeare

Titchfield Abbey

After the Dissolution of the Monasteries, the Earl of Southampton built a fine **Tudor Gatehouse** at Titchfield. It is said that several of Shakespeare's plays were performed here for the first time for his patron Henry Wriothesley (1573–1624) the 3rd Earl, and special favourite of Queen Elizabeth.

Portchester Castle lies on the south side of Portchester off the A27.
   Open daily 1 April–31 Oct
   10 am–6 pm; 1 Nov–31 March
   10 am–4 pm; (closed 24-26 Dec and
   1 Jan)

Titchfield Abbey lies ½ mile north of Titchfield off the A27.
   It can be viewed at any reasonable
   time.

47

INDEX

If you would like to join English Heritage write for details to:
English Heritage, PO Box 1BB, London W1A 1BB.

© I-Spy Limited 1995

ISBN (paperback) 1 85671 156 0

Michelin Tyre Public Limited Company
Edward Hyde Building, 38 Clarendon Road, Watford, Herts WD1 1SX

MICHELIN and the Michelin Man are Registered Trademarks of Michelin

Edited by Neil Curtis. Designed by Richard Garratt.

Consultant David Batchelor. The majority of illustrations in this I-Spy book are from the English Heritage Photographic Library, with additional photographs from Philip Craven, The Kennet and Avon Canal Trust, and The Great Western Railway Museum. The royal and other portraits are reproduced by kind permission of The National Portrait Gallery, London, except for the Brunel photograph courtesy of the Trustees of the Victoria and Albert Museum, the painting of King Arthur courtesy of Martspress Ltd.

Colour reproduction by Anglia Colour.

Printed in Spain by Graficromo.